Book 1
Drawing
By Scott Landowski

&

Book 2
Sculpting
By Scott Landowski

Book 1
Drawing

By Scott Landowski

1-2-3 Easy Techniques To Mastering Drawing

Drawing: 1-2-3 Easy Techniques to Mastering Drawing

Table of Contents

Introduction

I want to thank you and congratulate you for downloading the book, "Drawing: 1-2-3 Easy Techniques to Mastering Drawing".

This book contains proven steps and strategies on how to master drawing as a beginner artist. You will learn three basic techniques for sketching just about any subject you can think of. These are lines, shading and proportion - that's it!

Anyone can draw. They just need a bit of guidance to know how they can use simple lines and curves to capture the world on paper. There is an artist in each one of us and the tips in this book will help unleash him or her. Start with these techniques and you can move on to creating an art in any medium including painting and digital drawing.

What is important is that you have a good, solid foundation before experimenting with art. After that, you will only be limited by your imagination.

Thank again for downloading this book,   I hope you enjoy it!

Chapter 1 - Working with the Right Materials

Like with any other craft, drawing requires the right materials. It is best to choose artist grade and good quality tools, but there are also less expensive options at the art store that can give you real value for your money. Learn to experiment with various brands and types to find the ones that suit you and your drawing style best. There are many wonderful artists who can create beautiful works of art with simple and cheap art tools.

Pencils

Graphite Pencils

First, in order to begin sketching, you must have pencils. You cannot just have any pencil. You need to invest in those with different hardness. The most commonly used type of pencil in sketching is the graphite pencil. Others incorrectly refer to the grey graphite encased inside the wood as lead, when in fact, it has long been banned for use in pencils because it is toxic.

The hardness of a graphite pencil is denoted by a grade that ranges from 9B to 9H. The "B" stands for "black" or graphite that is softer, while "H" stands for graphite that is "harder." The B graphite looks darker while the H graphite is lighter. The HB graphite is the middle ground and it is an absolute must to have. It corresponds to the #2 pencil of more mainstream pencil brands. For sketching, it is often enough to have 5 different pencil grades at your disposal. That is enough to provide different tones and shadows to your drawing.

Other wood pencils can also have colored pigments, or what is pertained to as colored pencils. These, along with graphite pencils, are sharpened using a sharpener that fits the circumference of the pencil.

Mechanical Pencils

You can also use mechanical pencils. These come with barrels that you can refill with graphite of different diameters often denoted by a point millimeter size. You can push out the graphite by pressing a button without the need to sharpen the pencil. They are also excellent for drawing fine details as they retain their point and do not easily become blunt unlike wood pencils.

Pastels

Charcoal and chalk pastels produce colors that are more vivid. They are more blendable than graphite pencils and are also more difficult to control due to their size and softness.

Erasers

Erasers are also just as important as pencils. You can use them not just to correct errors, but to also add highlights and depth to your drawing. Avoid using the eraser found in the body of your pencil. It is often of poor quality and will cause your paper to tear easily. Also, due to its small size, you will quickly grind it down to the wood. A normal rubber eraser will be useful if you want to erase large areas, but you will realize that you will rarely need to do that. If you really do not like your work, it is best to start with a clean sheet of paper. Rubber erasers also create a lot of mess from the grit formed when rubbing them on paper with graphite.

The dust can affect your work and make it dirty. The kneaded artist eraser is much better because it takes off graphite marks without damaging the paper. The eraser lasts longer because rubber bits do not fall off when erasing. You can also erase in layers, which is useful if an area simply needs brightening or highlighting. You can further mold it smaller and pointier to do detail work. As well, a mechanical eraser can target small areas because of its size. You can even sharpen it with a craft knife to create a pointed eraser.

Blenders

Blending tools can help achieve more realistic drawings. The most common is a blending stump, which is a paper or felt cylinder that has been tightly rolled up with pointed ends. Q-tips also serve a similar purpose, but they are meant to be disposable and you cannot use one piece several times. Wads of cotton, paper napkins and fabrics can also be used as blending tools.

Ink

An alternative to sketching with pencils is to use ink. There are even more types of drawing pens than there are pencils. There are artist pens with different millimeter diameters. There are also different types of tips like fine, blunt or scroll (two-tipped). Brush pens, calligraphic pens, nib pens and even markers create various effects in drawing. You can also use a wet brush to spread the ink and color in your drawing. The downside to working with ink is that you can no longer erase your marks. Some artists prefer to draw in pencil first then trace over in ink.

Paper

Drawing paper can greatly affect the outcome of your drawing. However, your choice of brand all comes down to your personal preference. Some prefer paper with pronounced teeth for texture. The teeth refers to the grain of the paper. Pigments stick better to such paper, although the point of your drawing apparatus may also get caught on the teeth. On the other hand, there are those who prefer the look and feel of smoother paper. If you are overwhelmed by the number of paper choices at your disposal, then try to look for paper that was created precisely for pencil sketching.

Watercolor paper also usually makes a good medium for sketching. Avoid paper for acrylics or oils, as well as paper that is similar to fabric like felt and canvas. There are also drawing pads or journals that you can take with you as you travel. Some may prefer to just use notebooks with heavy paper stock for practice drawings.

If you want your drawings to last, you may also want to get a can of fixative. These are usually sprays and they help preserve your drawings. Over time, graphite may transfer or move on the paper, the paper may begin to age and moisture may start to affect the integrity of your drawing. A fixative acts as a protection from possible wear and tear. Think of it as a varnish or a top coat to seal in your work. Remember to purchase a fixative designed mainly for pencils or inks and not for other art media.

Chapter 2 - Warm Up Exercises

If you thought that warming up is just done before physical exercise, then you may be surprised to find out that you must also do warm ups before drawing. You do this to help loosen up your hand and allow you to practice your strokes before doing actual sketching.

Grip

First, warm up exercises help reorient you on how to hold your pencil properly. Many people are used to gripping their pencil for sketching the way they do for writing where it is nestled on top of the gap between their thumb and forefinger, so the bottom is pointing up. This is called the tripod grip. The best way to hold your pencil for sketching is to position it underneath the palm of your hand in what is called the overhand grip. This type of grip is looser and allows you bigger movement that comes from your entire arm rather than just your wrist. Also, you will not be smudging your paper because your hand hovers on top of the paper.

Doodles

Start by doing slanted lines. Quickly draw lines that move diagonally up then diagonally down. Do rows of this and draw them as fast as you can, then as close together as possible. Make them even and the same size every time.

Sketch hatches that are crossed horizontal and vertical lines.

Next, draw curved lines or Cs. Draw them forward, then in reverse. Just like the slanted lines, make them even and in rows.

From there, move on to doing spirals or ovals one on top of the other. Draw rows of perfect circles afterwards.

Draw 3D shapes. You can start by sketching cubes. Shade the exposed surfaces in different tones to practice your shading and shadows.

Sketch cylinders and bowls and shade them in using curved strokes, as well. Do the same for cones.

Contour Drawing

Also, do some contour drawing. Pick an object and draw its outline without lifting your pencil off your paper. This teaches you to pay attention to the shape of the object you are drawing. Some artists also like doing this exercise without looking at their paper, so their full attention is on the subject itself. If you want to have a bit more challenge, turn your back from your paper and draw without looking back. This is best done on a large paper like an A3 size. This exercise is what you call a blind contour.

Do not be occupied with making your warm up drawings perfect. You can just do them on scratch paper and sketch as many exercises as you want, although you also need to start practicing control. Remember that you are not simply doing. The warm up exercises are more purposeful than that and they will help you perform your strokes better later on when you are already doing actual sketches.

Chapter 3 - Choosing Subjects

Even though you want to draw abstract art or highly stylized figures, it is still important to learn how to draw objects realistically. This will teach you proper proportions and shadows. Once you have mastered realistic drawing, you will be able to break conventions and develop your own style.

Still Life

Beginner art classes usually start by sketching still life, which refers to small inanimate objects. You can just find random objects lying around your home or inside your bag. Try to find a combination of different textures, shapes and sizes. For example, a towel, bottle and fruits will allow you to practice drawing different types of objects. Also, make sure to arrange them in a way that they occupy different levels (i.e., high and low) and depths of fields (i.e., foreground, middle ground and background). This will teach you scale and perspective.

The most important thing to focus on when drawing still life is shape. For instance, an apple is just a circle with slight curves to make it look distinct from an orange. Likewise, a bottle is just a cylinder while a towel is just a polygonal shape. Once you can see shapes in real life, then it will be easier to capture how objects look in your sketches.

From small objects, you can move on to larger things like furniture or even entire rooms. The practice in perspective will also help you transition to doing landscapes.

Landscape

What is most important in landscape is perspective. You may have seen landscape paintings where most of the details are blurred. This is completely understandable, because when you are drawing something vast like a mountain view or an urban jungle, you won't be able to draw all the small parts. The observer won't notice these in real life when they are looking at the bigger picture. However, when there is something off with your perspective, then the illusion of realism is shattered.

For example, a tree close to the viewer should be bigger than a large mountain that is miles away. Amateur artists who do not pay attention to what they can actually see in the world may not realize this because in real life, trees are much smaller than mountains, but sometimes, what you think is logical does not really match reality.

Figure Drawing

This is especially true when drawing people. You may instinctively think that your leg is longer than your arm when they are actually the same length. Your ears are also not high on your head but right in the middle of it at the same level as your nose.

Some artists start with statues, so you can go to an art gallery or a park where there are busts and sculptures. Look for subjects with realistic proportions. Again, focus on the shapes that you can find in a human body. The head is a circle while the limbs are cylinders. Spend more time on getting the actual figure or overall shape of the subject before learning how to draw the fingers, toes and facial features. Portraits or faces are typically the last type of drawings that artists master.

Next, you can practice drawing actual people. You can have a model sit down for a session or discreetly draw strangers sitting down in a public place.

There are places that offer figure drawing sessions with professional models. Some do nude modeling, which is beneficial for artists who want to understand fully how the human body looks.

Gesture Drawing

Gesture drawings are done quickly, usually in short intervals of 15, 30 or 60 seconds, with the use of expressive lines and shapes. They serve as starting points for different genres of art that do not rely on hyper-realistic figures like impressionism. Gesture drawings focus on the basic form and proportion of a subject and record that without much emphasis on details. They are good for practicing speed and expressing movement in drawing. Erasing is rarely done and mistakes give the drawing even more character.

The subject of a gesture drawing can be any object in motion like moving persons, animals, cars, boats and toys. The best place to find subjects is outdoors where there are lots of activities. You can watch a busy intersection and try to draw different kinds of people walking about and dodging cars. In a park, you can draw joggers with their dogs or children playing with their toys.

Chapter 4 - Easy Technique 1 - Lines

For any drawing that you do, you can start with an H pencil to create light outlines and follow up with a B pencil for the darker, more defined lines. However, you can also simply use just one pencil and vary your pressure as you draw more layers of lines. Also, the point of your pencil, especially when freshly sharpened, will create thin, light lines.

On the other hand, the side of your pencil will create thick, dark lines. You can also make the point blunt by rubbing it on another piece of paper. If you want to just use one pencil, instead of switching between H and B pencils, then use an HB or #2 pencil as described in Chapter 1.

So, your drawing should have at least two layers of lines: the first light outline, which you can use as a guideline to capture the basic shapes of the subject, and thicker lines on top of that to form the rest of your drawing.

For the first layer of lines, try to use a light pressure when pressing down on your pencil and use only light strokes. The fainter you make the lines, the better. They will be easier to erase later on if you have to.

The layer on top of the outline will use heavy lines. You can trace over the light outline, then vary your pressure and strokes as you go along to create more definition to your figure. Define the edges and the details. At this point, you want to be more careful as erasing may be more difficult to do on thick, dark lines. Even if you can lift the marks off your paper, the indentations may still be obvious and they may show up more if you draw over them.

You can also go over your final pencil outlines with ink and erase the pencil lines for a more polished look.

In drawing, it is impossible to create perfectly straight lines, so do not worry if your tables or boxes have crooked edges. The only way to achieve truly straight lines is to use a ruler, although dragging or rolling your pencil on its edge, instead of using the point, will help achieve straighter lines. Also, imperfect lines give your drawings more life and expression. Perfectly straight lines are also difficult to find in nature and in real life. Even buildings or straight poles have curves and small dips on their edges. That is why a drawing that makes use of straight lines looks cold, stiff and lifeless. It looks rather unrealistic and uninteresting.

Lines and Values

Drawings are made up of lines and clusters of lines or values. Lines are the flowing strokes of a pencil that define edges or small details while values are used to define the form and design of a drawing. Using both will give your drawings character.

The term value is sometimes used interchangeably with the terms "shade", "tint" and "tone." These terms are most useful when working with colored pencils.

Shade refers to the color achieved when black is combined with a pure color. You can do this to darken colors. For example, ultramarine, navy blue and midnight blue are shades of blue.

Tint refers to the color achieved when white is combined with a pure color. You can do this to lighten colors. For example, pink, rose and coral are tints of red.

Tone refers to the color achieved when grey is combined with a pure color. For example, khaki, brown and gold are tones of yellow.

However, when drawing with grey graphite pencils, these will all just fall under "value." Knowing if a color is a shade, tint or tone will allow you to adjust the values in your drawings to depict the color of your subject even in a black and white drawing. You simply need to look at the darkness or lightness of the greys you are using. A pink-colored blouse will look like a light grey while dark blue denim jeans will look almost black.

Furthermore, take note that value is different from the concept of shading, which will be discussed in Chapter 4. So for this chapter, only look at the "color" of the lines you are making

Value Scale

A value scale is extremely helpful to beginner artists. This will serve as a guide so you can tell what value you can use for different parts of your drawing. Most find a ten-point value scale to be adequate. You can make one on a piece of paper by drawing ten circles or squares. Fill the first one with the lightest stroke you can create with your pencil or with your lightest pencil. Next, fill the last one with the darkest stroke you can create with your pencil or with your darkest pencil.

Fill the rest with the remaining values in between going from the lightest to the darkest value. Use this scale as a guide that you can compare parts of your drawing to, so the heaviest outline should match the last value while faint edges should match the first value. Medium colors should match the two middle values.

By using values, you can also adjust the contrast of your drawing. A high contrast drawing will make more use of values at each end of the spectrum - almost black to almost white. Low contrast drawings will use a good mix of the whole spectrum. Whichever variation in value that you choose is completely up to you and will depend on the effect that you want to achieve. Your drawing can be harsh, bold and solid or soft, faint and hazy.

Thick and Thin Lines

The quickest way to achieve various values in your drawing is to vary the thickness of your lines. Thin lines represent the light values while thick lines represent the dark values. You can get different thicknesses by simply varying your pressure, using pencil points with different dullness, or using different pencils.

Scribbling

Scribbling is a good way to fill a space with a lot of values in a short period of time. It is quick and you can create hundreds of strokes in a minute. More advanced artists can create drawings made up of just scribbles and the subject will still remain clear to the viewer. Beginner artists may try this technique and just end up with a bunch of scribbles that do not look like anything. Again, focusing on the shape of the subject will give you a general guideline for where to lay down the scribbles on your paper.

You do scribbling by drawing a continuous series of lines that go in different directions. The sensation you should feel when scribbling is comparable to writing in longhand or cursive. Control the value by varying speed, pressure and distance between the scribbles. For example, when doing a portrait using the scribbling technique, the dark and closely overlapping scribbles will be concentrated on the subject's features like his hair, eyebrows, eyes, nose, mouth and general outline of the face.

Some scribbles may be used to define cheekbones, the sides of the nose and around the mouth where shadows fall on the face. Lastly, very faint scribbles can depict highlights on the face like the apples of the cheeks, the pupil and whites of the eyes, and shine of the lips and hair.

Side Strokes

Side strokes is a favorite among sketchers who do fast and loose drawings. They are especially good for achieving different values than for plain contour drawings. Short, sideways strokes will create different values of greys depending on the pressure, closeness of the lines and overlapping.

Wide Strokes

Wide strokes are good if you want to try getting a general impression of a subject. You use big, long (not necessarily dark) lines. Whereas side strokes are short lines, wide strokes take up more space in a short period of time. So, they are often used for large subjects like the full figure of a person or a wide landscape. You can also use them when getting the general movement or shape of a large portion of the drawing such as the drape of a fabric or hair flowing in the wind. It takes a lot of confidence to achieve wide strokes because it can sometimes make or break the foundation of your entire drawing.

Charcoal pencils or pastels are great to use when trying to achieve wide strokes, because these take less effort to get broad lines. They also go on paper smoothly and don't catch on the "teeth" of the paper, which sometimes happens when drawing wide strokes with graphite pencils.

Single Strokes

Single strokes are simply straight lines drawn in a row. This is best done with a sharp pencil and each area is filled with parallel lines. Values are achieved by varying the density of the lines or how close the group of lines are to each other. The farther away the lines are, the lighter the value. It is a refined technique and is not as loose as the previous types of line drawings. It does create a similar effect with scribbling, except more polished.

However, it takes precision because one line that is not in its right place or a bit more crooked than the other will easily stand out and catch the attention of the viewer. Beginner artists should practice using this technique just to learn patience and meticulousness in drawing. It is good to use as a counter-balance to other stroke techniques. It is also best used for drawings that require precision like architecture.

Smudging and Erasing

After scribbling or doing side strokes, you can smudge the lines with your finger or other blender tools mentioned in Chapter 1. This will soften or smoothen the harsh lines. It is also a good technique to use when trying to achieve medium values. However, some artists avoid this technique because it does not teach how to achieve values properly using only lines. Also, smudging can get quite messy, which can ruin an already good drawing. It may be a form of cheating, but when done right or with some caution, you can enhance the drawing.

Another way to achieve lighter values is by erasing. This creates highlights or contrasting definition to some parts of a drawing. Sometimes, it is easier to just erase a portion filled with darker values than to avoid drawing on that spot or trying to achieve the lightest value you can.

Chapter 5 - Easy Technique 2 - Shading

Shading is another important technique in drawing. They give your sketches life and depth because they mimic the light and shadows found in the real world.

The progression of shading or values from light to dark or dark to light are called graduations. Graduated shading is important so that there is a good transition from one value to another. Beginner artists may jump from one value to another without proper graduation and this creates harsh, unrealistic shadows in their drawings. This is only acceptable when one is trying to create an obvious contrast between different portions of a drawing. For instance, the edge of an object should be distinguishable from its background; otherwise, the object will disappear.

Graduations can be done through a variation of strokes, pressure or pencil hardness. Continuously adjust the changes in values so that the transitions are not apparent. There should be no demarcations or borders that separate two or more values in a graduated shading. Adjust any areas that look irregular.

If you are just starting to experiment with graduation in drawing, you should being from the lightest shading to the darkest. It is much easier to build up on the color of a grey pencil than it is to remove an already dark color to make it lighter.

Light Source

Always identify where the light source of your subject is. When you do not consider where the light is coming from, your drawing will look two dimensional. For example, when drawing an outdoor scene, take note of where the sun is depending on the time of day. Noon time creates solid shadows that are short and go straight down from the objects. The lower the sun in the sky is (especially at the beginning and at the end of the day), the longer and fainter the shadows are. They will also slant at different directions. When it comes to drawing still life indoors, take notice of where the window is or where a light fixture is in a room - those are your possible sources of light.

Use the light as a guide where to draw shading, so a circle can transform in a sphere. Amateur artists will just place shadows and highlights where they think it looks good, so then, the drawing will turn out looking wrong. It is not as simple as coloring in a drawing, especially when only working with grey pencils.

A drawing can also have multiple sources of light. The closer or stronger the light source is, the darker the shadows and the lighter the highlights will be. That is another reason why artists should start with drawing objects from the real world. Understanding how light affects how an object looks is important in accurately capturing it on paper. Always pay close attention to the object you are drawing, including the different factors that surround it.

Highlighting

Highlights are parts of an object where bright areas form as a light hits it. The part, which is most directly hit by the light source will then be the brightest, thus, you need to shade them with light values. This should be the portion closest to the light. An apple directly under a light bulb will have a highlight on its top portion that graduates as you move down to the bottom of the apple where you will find the shadow. As such, highlights accentuate the form of an object because it can depict where an object bulges or where parts of it protrude.

In portrait drawings, the highlights are often found on the tip of the nose, the apples of the cheeks, the forehead, the chin and the Cupid 's bow. The texture of an object will also affect how highlights look on it. For instance, shiny surfaces like glass, water or a person's eyes will catch light better than coarser surfaces like sand, carpeting or wood. Also, the color of an object affects how well it can reflect light back to the viewer.

Light-colored or white-colored objects generally reflect light better while dark-colored objects absorb light, so light green leaves on a tree will have lighter highlights than the dark wood of its trunk. However, the contrast between the highlight and the rest of the object can also be more apparent in dark-colored objects. For instance, highlight on brunette hair is more obvious than on blond hair.

The value of a highlight also varies depending on the type of highlight that an object receives. A highlight formed from the direct light of a source should be bright. However, highlights can also form from indirect reflections or bouncing of light around the object. For example, the shiny surface of an apple can bounce a tiny bit of light on objects surrounding it. Their highlights will be faint, but these should still be depicted to create more realistic representations of the objects.

Casting Shadows

Shadows are found in the parts of a drawing that receive the least amount of light. It can also be found when parts of an object block the light such as in creases and dips. Things surrounding that object can also block light or cast a shadow depending on the angle that the light is coming from. These are then shaded with the darker values, so the top of an apple right under a bright light will still have dark shading where you can find the stem. In portrait drawings, shadows can be found on the parts of the face obscured by hair, the inside of the mouth, the cheekbones, under the eyebrows and eyes, and the creases in the ears, around the eyes and mouth.

Just like in highlighting, the natural color and texture of an object will also affect the shadows that form on it. For example, a long-haired fur coat on a dog will create a lot of small shadows where the tiny hairs are located. The shadow on a black t-shirt will also have to be much darker than when drawing shadows on a white t-shirt where it more easily shows up.

A shadow should also be graduated and should not simply appear as black shading. The portions of a shadow farther away from where an object obstruct light should be lighter, so the long shadow of a tree will be darkest near the roots and fade to a lighter value as it moves away from the roots. This also suggests the placement of objects in your drawing and creates the illusion of depth and perspective.

Shadows also suggest the parts of objects that are touching or are close to one another. Instead of drawing sharp edges, an object's edges can be more realistically depicted through the use of shadows.

Reflected light also affects how shadows look. The form of an object can be further enhanced by looking at where light is reflected from other objects. This goes in tandem with highlighting. Once you understand how highlighting and shadowing works, you can create three dimensional realities in your drawings.

Hatching

Hatching is a set of straight or curved lines drawn in a series beside each other to achieve a particular value. This is a common shading technique and is the easiest to master. That is because you are only working with one set of hatches. The density of the hatches will create the effect that you want, so hatching sets close to one another will look darker while hatching sets that are far apart will look lighter. Very close hatching lines will create the illusion of a solid value or color.

The hatches can also be short or long depending on the area that the artist wants to cover. For example, a shadow cast by a pine tree will form a triangular shape. So, the hatches can be a series of short and long lines that form the rough shape of a triangle. Hatching is also commonly used to draw straight hair or fur.

You can achieve graduation by changing the thickness of the lines and the distances between them. The principle is similar to some stroke techniques discussed in the previous chapter.

Crosshatching

Crosshatching is a type of hatching where the hatching sets are laid on top of one another as if creating crosses. When you overlap two or more hatching sets, you can create darker values. However, crosshatched sets with hatching sets that are far apart will show up as lighter values. The form of crosshatched sets usually follows the shape of an object to depict creases and textures. It is often used to show shadows on an object and does not have to rely on an outline. The spaces in between the hatches can be apparent or they can look like a solid shade depending on the effect that the artist wants to achieve.

Scribbling

Scribbling can also be a shading technique, especially when used in overlapping sets to create different values. It is a versatile technique that you can use to create shading on textures like curly hair, grassy fields or fuzzy cloth. The texture of scribbles can be adjusted to depict the smoothness or roughness of a surface. Scribbles and be a series of squiggles, entwined circles or irregular continuous lines. When used properly by more advanced artists, scribbling can still look quite polished rather than look like a random, unfinished doodle.

Dots

Dots are technically small lines or points. You can use them for shading through a variation of density and pressure. In essence, a densely grouped set of heavily drawn dots will look darker than a group of light dots drawn far apart. It does take a longer time to shade using dots than with other shading techniques, but the payoff can well be worth it. The illusion can be interesting for the viewer especially for larger art pieces. The nearer the viewer is, the more he or she will be able to appreciate the effort that went into the drawing.

A type of drawing that uses dots exclusively is called pointillism. Every dot is laid dot one by one to create lines, forms and shapes.

You can also cheat with this technique by holding several pencils together to draw multiple dots at the same time. It may be less precise, but it does cover more area in a shorter period of time. This technique is sometimes called stippling.

Chapter 6 - Easy Technique 3 - Proportion

Proportion is another important element of any good drawing. Many drawings with good lines and shading still look odd because they do not follow the right proportions. Think of a room filled with people. You may think that all the people in that room are the same size, so you will draw them that way. However, a room is not a flat like a piece of paper. People will stand in different places with some closer to the viewer than others, so those who are closest to you should look bigger than those standing in farther parts of the room.

Also, their sizes and shapes will depend on which direction of the room you are looking towards. If you are looking slightly upwards to the ceiling while sitting down on the floor, then the people's legs will look bigger than their heads, even though common sense dictates that legs should be smaller than heads. This distortion is due to different factors that affect proportion.

Depth of field

Any three dimensional drawing will have different depths of field. There should at least be a foreground, middle ground and background and objects should be found on these different levels. This tricks the viewer's eye into thinking that he or she is not looking at a flat piece of paper but rather, a 3-dimensional picture.

As such, the placement of objects on these different levels of depth of field will affect their size and shape. The objects closest to the viewer should appear biggest while the objects farthest from the viewer should appear smallest. Their sizes relative to one another in the drawing will also be affected by the distances between these levels and the actual sizes of the objects. For instance, a large mountain can still appear quite large even when it is in the background of a drawing, granted that the distance of the mountain is not that far from the viewer. A bird in the foreground will still look quite small compared to other objects in a landscape drawing because birds really are small in real life.

Foreshortening

Foreshortening refers to the shortening of an object as it moves towards the viewer. For instance, imagine a person with one arm by his side and another arm reaching out towards you. The arms on an average person should be the same length, but when drawing arms at different distances from the viewer, the arm closer to you should look shorter but bigger. This suggests that the arm is in the foreground while the other arm is located farther in the drawing.

The same principle applies when drawing any object that occupies different depths of field. For instance, you may be drawing a picture of a car from its front. The front of the car including its hood, front window and headlights should look big but short while its rear end should taper longer and look smaller.

By using foreshortening, you can also create the illusion of using different "lenses" in your drawing much like in photography. For example, a fish eye lens distorts an image in such a way that the center is larger and shorter than the rounded edges. You can use this when drawing reflections on concave surfaces like balls or windows or when depicting objects inside glasses like fishbowls and eyeglasses.

Similarly, wide-angle lenses also distort an image so that the central objects look large and shortened compared to the sides. You can use this technique when trying to depict objects that should look extremely close to the viewer like a very close-up shot of a person's face or a focal building surrounded by other minor buildings in an urban landscape.

Focal Point

The focal point is also important to consider when trying to get the perspective of a drawing correctly. This is the point where the viewer's eye is focused. Understand that your eyes can only point in one direction and on only one spot in a scene. That is why there are points in a scene that we call blind spots - spots that your eyes cannot see. To create realistic drawings, you can also mimic the illusion of peripheral vision.

To find the focal point of a drawing, just choose one spot to focus on in a scene. This can be found on any level of depth of field. However, beginner artists may want to start with a focal point somewhere in the middle ground or foreground and somewhere to one side of the scene. In a room, this can be the corner of one of the far walls. In a landscape, this can be the tip of a mountain. Also, take note that your focal point will be the focus of your drawing. It is one part where the eyes of the viewer will be drawn to, so choose a significant portion of the scene, usually one where the main subject is located.

Next, imagine lines radiating from that focal point. You can also draw these lines as your first layer of outlines as explained in Chapter 4. These lines will serve as guidelines for foreshortening your objects. Lines that radiate farther apart from one another should have shorter and bigger objects while lines that radiate closer to each other should contain longer and smaller objects.

Finding the focal point is much easier when drawing large scenes that contain different objects. It is a lot harder when drawing single subject accompanied by not a lot of objects. Sometimes, the focal point is already that one subject. This usually happens in portrait drawings, so just focus on one striking detail on the person's face like the lips or eyes then use shading and highlighting to emphasize that feature. It is always better to draw the viewer's gaze to one point in the drawing than to have a lot of things going on in a picture.

Grid Method

For more accurate perspectives and scale, you can try the grid method when drawing. The grid method involves drawing as grid or a series of squares that will serve as guide when you are drawing a subject. These squares are of equal ratio and can be part of your first layer of outlines. They are usually erased before the drawing is finalized.

You can draw a rough grid on your paper by first finding the middle. Draw a vertical line and a horizontal line that meets in the middle of the paper, then divide the rest of the paper into equal parts. You can also use a ruler or straight edge to create a more precise guide. Some people may prefer to fold their paper in equal parts to create a sort of invisible grid without drawing any lines on the paper. However, you may find that the folds on the paper can still be distracting and may make it difficult to draw lines and shading more smoothly. This trick is best done on thin paper where folds can be smoothed out.

Then, imagine these lines over the subject you are drawing. They will allow you to find the correct placement of objects as well as their proper proportions relative to one another. It is best to start in the middle of the scene and work your way around the rest of the image. You are essentially filling out each box with a part of the image much like a jigsaw puzzle being put together. Be aware of the whole image that you are producing because if you focus on individual portions of the drawing without considering the bigger picture, the parts may end up looking disjointed.

This technique is especially useful in portrait drawings because the average human face has perfect proportions. The middle of the grid will be the nose and the eyes and mouth are located on equal distances from the nose.

Your grid does not necessarily have to be flat. It can also form the shape of a sphere as when drawing a round human head or a globe. Images that form cylinders or other curved objects will also benefit from a more spherical grid. The middle of spherical grids can be a straight line if the viewer is looking the image straight on or a curved line if the viewer is looking at an angle.

The grid technique is also used in image transfers. This is another exercise that beginner artists can try. You can do this by taking a printed photo and drawing a grid over the image, then try copying the image by drawing a similar grid on your paper and simply sketching the image as an exact replica of the photograph. This may not teach you how to draw realistically because you are drawing from another flat image, but it will teach you how to make use of the grid technique. It is also great when you want to simply copy other two-dimensional images like cartoons or letterings.

Over time and after a lot of practice, you can simply imagine the grid on your paper without having to draw it as an outline.

Conclusion

Thank you again for downloading this book!

I hope this book was able to help you to master basic techniques in drawing and help you on your way to becoming an advanced artist who experiments with different media and art genres.

The next step is to practice, practice and practice! That is the only way you can be a better artist. Try out every single tip you encountered in this book and draw wherever you can - at home, in a café, or out on the street. In no time, you will find that you rarely even think of these "rules" anymore and the lines, shading and proportion comes naturally to you as an artist.

Finally, if you enjoyed this book, please take the time to share your thoughts and post a review on Amazon. It'd be greatly appreciated!

Thank you and good luck!

Book 2
Sculpting

By Scott Landowski

1-2-3 Easy Techniques to Mastering Sculpting

Sculpting: 1-2-3 Easy Techniques to Mastering Sculpting

Table of Contents

Introduction

Introduction

I want to thank you and congratulate you for downloading the book, "Sculpting: 123 Easy Techniques for Mastering Sculpting".

This book contains proven steps, strategies, and techniques on how to master the art of making and creating different types of wood, stone and metal sculptures.

Through the centuries, all major works of art, especially sculptures, were produced because a client asked the artist to work on it via a *direct commission* or through a *competition*. Although these days, the production of sculptures has evolved to include the artists taking the initiative to create sculpted pieces of art and then exhibiting them to the public to sell, the stages of production that every sculpture should go through has not changed much through the ages.

Time and again producing a sculpture goes through this process:

The artist is commissioned to do the work. Initial designs are submitted by the artist for approval of the client. When the design is approved, the artist then selects the specific materials to be used for the creation of the sculpture. After that, the materials are prepared and shaped into the form envisioned in the plans the artist has drawn. Once the artist is satisfied with the form of the sculpture, it undergoes surface finishing. This is the final flourish to the sculpture. Then and only then the sculpture can be installed and presented to the client or to the public for viewing.

This book will discuss in detail the middle part of the process. The many techniques artists employ in creating and shaping all sorts of materials into a sculpture and a work of art.

Thanks again for downloading this book, I hope you enjoy it!

Chapter 1: Carving Techniques

In this chapter, we will discuss one of the many age old methods or techniques artists use to create a sculpture and that technique is called *carving*. There are two ways of creating this kind of sculpture: the first is through *direct carving* and the second *indirect carving*.

Direct Carving

The most common materials used for *direct carving* are wood, marble, granite and almost all types of metal. *Direct carving* is a reductive process. It entails reducing the mass of a solid piece of wood, stone or metal into a shape or form the artist has envisioned. In the process of *direct carving* the sculptor removes solid chunks of wood, stone or metal from the original slab he or she has chosen to work on to arrive at a shape or form desired.

Once the block of material is carved into an initial desired shape, the sculptor then starts to chisel, cut, or saw tiny little bits off from the sculpted material to give it its final, more detailed form. If, for example, the artist wants to sculpt a human form, the details would be the accurate parts of the human body such as eyes, mouth, hair, ear, arms, legs etc. After this detail work is accomplished, the artist then decides on the finishing touches for the final texture or color of the sculpture.

Direct carving is a very tactile and evolved process of creating a piece of art. This is especially true at the latter part of the process when it is almost completed, which is the stage where the specific artistic details are added by the sculptor to the sculpture.

Often in the beginning of the sculpting process, the sculptor will ask a craftsman or an apprentice to shape the block of material for him so that it resembles the form that he wants. When this is accomplished he steps in and works on the grueling detail work himself. This attention to detail often defines the sculpture as a work of art. This is the reason creating a sculpture is a very personal and organic creative process for the artist.

Indirect Carving

In the early 19th century, another form of carving evolved called *indirect carving*. It is a bit of an involved process since it requires the final form or shape to be molded into a clay model first and then using the *pointing method* the shape is indirectly carved into another surface.

The *indirect carving* method is not as popular as direct carving. Artists and sculptors find the process less than appealing compared to direct carving. It is deemed as more creative for the artist to be able to work on, touch, feel and shape a piece of wood, stone and metal into a work of art. Direct carving allows artists to do that while indirect carving not so much.

It is not unusual therefore that through the years *direct carving* has overtaken *indirect carving* as the preferred carving method artists use to create sculptures.

Tools for Carving

The tools and techniques used for carving differ depending on the material that is being used to produce a sculpture. This is because the malleability of wood, stone and metal surfaces differs. Nonetheless, there are also certain sets of tools that are applicable to all sculpting surface materials with a few tweaks and nuances.

Some of the basic tools used for stone sculptures are:

a. *Pitcher chisels:* It has a wide beveled edge that breaks the stone instead of cutting it. It looks like a thick chisel. Both ends of the pitcher chisel are used to hammer into the surface of the stone so that it can be broken off into chips. It is the preferred tool at the onset of the sculpting process when a craftsman starts shaping a block of wood, stone or metal into a shape.

b. *Claw chisels:* It is similar in shape to the pitcher chisels except that it has a toothed edge. Claw chisels are used to refine the surface form after the pitcher chisel has done its work. This is the tool used in the second stage of the sculpting process after chunks of wood, stone or metal has been removed from the block of original material.

c. *Flat chisels:* With its sharp edge, flat chisels are great for adding the finishing touches to the surface of the final shape of the sculpture. It is used to polish the surface further and shape it into a more distinct form.

d. *Gouges:* For the detail work on the surface, gouges are the best tools to use. To create a face or a texture on a stone surface a sculptor would use a gouge to achieve the intended detail. To create a pair of eyes on a stone surface, a gouge is the tool to use, for example.

e. *Drills:* Whereas gouges are manual tools, drills are power tools used for the same purpose as gouges –for detail work on a stone surface.

f. *Toothed Hammers:* These are similar in form to hammers except that both ends are toothed instead of flat. Used for creating texture on the stone surface.

g. *Abrasions:* Much like sandpaper for wood surfaces, abrasions allow a sculptor to achieve a smooth surface and rounded edges on any stone surface.

Tools for wood sculptures:

a. *Saw:* This is used to remove chunks of wood in the process of creating a shape or form from the wood slab.

b. *Axe:* In the same manner as a saw is utilized, an axe allows the sculptor to remove chunks or blocks of wood from the wood slab the sculpture will be shaped from.

c. *Wood gouges:* For the detail work, wood gouges are used to refine the wood form so that it reflects the shape or form the artist intends it to have. If a face for example, wood gouges are used to create the eyes, nose, and ears. All the features that make up a face.

d. *Sand paper:* Once the final sculpture form and detail work is completed. Polishing is the next step. Sand paper is the tool used to polish and refine the texture of any wood surface.

e. *Mallets:* These are the hammers that the artist or craftsman uses to drive in the gouges and other tools into the wood sculpture.

Chapter 2: Modeling Techniques

If carving involves reducing a block of wood, stone or metal into a certain shape or form, *modeling* is the opposite. It involves building up from scratch the form or shape the artist desires. The preferred modeling materials sculptors use to create sculptures are clay, wax, plaster, molten plaster, wax, molten metal, resin, or plastic wood.

Casting

Casting is the most common form of modeling sculpture. The technique dates to the time of the pharaohs in Egypt where ancient Egyptians would build actual houses using clay.

Through the ages *casting with clay* has evolved into a favored sculpting technique used by artists for generations everywhere in the world. The process of casting with clay is a special one in that it involves using a core called an *armature*.

An armature is the skeleton of the final form of the sculpture. The sculptor builds it so that the clay can be added to the armature or skeleton to build mass and eventually achieve the shape intended. If the sculptor wants to cast a clay model of two horses pouncing on each other for, he will first need to build an armature or the skeletal shape of the two horses pouncing.

Without an armature, it is nearly impossible to create a clay cast of any form. The armature is also a crucial component because once the casting of the clay begins, it will not be possible to change the shape or form of the armature. The armature defines the final form of the sculpture. The artist understands it is important to finalize the shape of the armature first before starting clay casting. Armatures are often made up of a mix of welded metal, concrete and pieces of wood.

Another form of casting is called *metal casting.* In contrast to clay casting, metal casting requires a bit more work and is a more involved process than the former. This is because liquid metal is a special sculpting material that requires special care and thought to use in sculpting.

Often, a plaster model is required to cast the metal form in. This means the sculptor starts with creating an armature where plaster can be added into to create the shape of the final metal cast. However, since in the final process the interior of the metal cast sculpture needs to be hollowed out, the core of the sculpture, which is the armature, should be of a certain material that can be removed from within the final metal cast. Often, armatures for *metal casting* are made of clay and not metal and wood which are more difficult to remove from inside the metal cast.

Sculpting: 1-2-3 Easy Techniques to Mastering Sculpting

Tools for Casting

Some of the basic materials used for casting are: moulage, paste maker, plaster, hydrocal casting, pliatex casting filler, and pliatex casting rubber. The tools used for making casts are: plaster mixing bowls, mold dividing shim, mold makers knife, carving chisel, plaster rasp, single wire end modeling tool, and mold making key knife.

For the armature, although the artists can build them using wood or steel. The preferred material artists use for armatures is the very sturdy aluminum wire. They have been proven to be non-corrosive and fully pliable; they do not stain, and are lightweight enough to work with. The choice of material for the armature or the skeleton of the sculpture is very important because it will determine the longevity of the sculpture.

Pottery Sculpture

Another form of clay modeling or clay casting is *pottery sculpture*. There are two ways of creating pottery sculpture: *hollow modeling* and *solid modeling*.

Hollow modeling of clay sculptures involves the traditional techniques of making pottery. Clay is set in a pottery wheel and as the clay is spun it is pinched, slabbed, coiled, and formed into the shape preferred. Once the sculptor is satisfied with the basic shape the exterior details are added. The clay then is removed from the pottery wheel and goes through the final stages of drying and firing.

The other pottery sculpture technique is called *solid modeling*. Using a solid mass of clay, the sculptor works on it to achieve a desired form. It is not unusual for an artist to use an armature for solid clay modeling. Once the clay is modeled to perfection, it is cut open, the armature is removed, and then dried and fired up in the kiln.

Modeled sculptures are characterized by three things; they are shaped by an interior form, there is more freedom of shape because they are not limited by the original form of the material they are created from, and they are more open to artistic manipulation than carved sculptures.

Tools for Pottery Sculpture

Artists use sculpting tools to perform the following tasks: cut, scrape, shape, smooth, and add detail. Sculpting tools are often very numerous and each one performs a specific function for the artist. This is the reason sculpting tools always come in sets. Some of the sculpting tools available to artists are: wire end modeling set, hard wood modeling & scraping set, carbon steel sculpting set, stainless steel shaping tools, modeling spatula sets to name a few.

Chapter 3: Constructing Techniques

Also, referred to as *assemblage,* constructed sculpture is the bringing together of certain pieces of material to create a work of art. Assemblage is in stark contrast with carving and modeling because the former two sculpting techniques require the artist to create a form using a block of wood, stone or metal.

Assemblage on the other hand uses pre-formed components such as metal tube, wood, bars, plates, timber, Formica, glass, wires, threads, etc. to create the sculpture. There is in fact almost no limits to the materials a sculptor can use in the process of creating a constructed or assembled sculpture. Any found material for if it can be assembled into a certain shape or form can be material for this kind of sculpture.

Another contrast between carving/modeling & *assemblage* is the materials used for *assemblage* retain their form in the process of building a new form. We can see for example steel rods, wires, glass are welded together to create an *assemblage* of the human form.

With assembled sculpture, we see both the shape of the materials as well as the shape of the sculpture which are often not the same. Assemblage is often a shape or form arrived at using the shapes and forms of assembled materials.

Assemblage sculptures are created using a combination of crafts and traditional sculpting techniques. Depending on the materials used assembled or constructed sculpture are created by welding, screwing, riveting, nailing, gluing, wood joinery, etc.

Assemblage has gained popularity in the 20th century until the present because the final artwork looks more modern than carved and modeled sculpture. Constructed sculpture lends itself to be more in tune with the times and the symbolisms it creates are congruent with the current technology-driven age.

Tools for Assemblage

The basic tools for creating *assemblage* are numerous. Since *assemblage* involve the processes of welding, screwing, nailing etc. The following are just some of the tools used to create this sculpture:

1. *Welding machine:* The main equipment used for welding metals together is the welding machine.

2. *Cutting Torch:* The cutting torch allows the sculptor to cut through a solid metal surface using intense heat.

3. *Grinder:* The tool used for removing rust, deburring rust, polishing and cutting materials made of metal is the grinder.

4. *Chipping hammer:* With a dual bevel tail and a sharp flattened point, the chipping hammer is used to remove slag and clean off welded metal.

5. *Wire brush:* A brush made of wood or plastic with thin wires that serve as a cleaning tool. It is used to clean and prepare the metal that is going to be welded to make sure it is not contaminated with unwanted layers of excess materials.

6. *Hand file:* A long textured metal tool that is used to smooth rough and coarse edges of brass and steel sometimes even wooden edges.

7. *Vise grips & pliers:* These are the tools to use if the artist requires a piece of metal to be locked in position while it is being welded in an *assemblage*. Vise grips are like pliers, one side includes a bolt that is adjustable and allows it to be a locking plier.

8. *Clamps:* These are *assemblage* tools that are used to secure objects firmly to any surface or together to prevent separation and movement. This is very useful for constructed sculpture which often uses an array of materials to create a whole.

9. *Adjustable wrench:* A wrench with a jaw that is adjustable. This allows the artist to fasten it to a metal object that is part of the assemblage and move it or adjust its position in the constructed sculpture.

10. *Safety gear:* These are a set of personal protective gear that covers important parts of the body or even the entire body while the artist is welding, creating or building an *assemblage*. Safety gears include hard hats, hand gloves, welding eyeglasses, ear guards, industrial boots, etc.

Chapter 4: Metal Sculpting Techniques

Direct Metal Sculpture

Welding and forging are techniques used for direct metal sculpture. This is a new technique that was introduced by the Spanish sculptor Julio Gonzalez in the 30s. It was adopted by other European and American artists in the 40s and 50s and has since been used by many artists to this day as their preferred form of sculpting.

Direct metal sculpture was made possible by the invention of the *oxyacetylene welding torch*. If not for this metal work equipment artists would not have been able to create metal sculpture as a new sculpting technique. Technology has always influenced the evolution of art, and the *oxyacetylene welding torch* is a prime example of that.

Welding

An art form that is created using the technique of *welding* is referred to as welded sculpture. The process involves cutting and joining together pieces of metal using a welding torch. Although steel is the most common metal used for welding virtually any kind of metal can be welded together to create a metal sculpture. Welding emerged in the beginning of the industrial age when steel and other hard metal were discovered and invented.

For industries to use the new metals it was necessary to invent a new technology that will allow them to build with steel. Welding was that new technology. Artists of the times understood that there was an opportunity to use the same new technology and the same new metals to create art. This is the reason welded sculptures or metal sculptures started to emerge as a new art form at the beginning of the industrial revolution.

Brazing

The process of joining together two different kinds of metal using an alloy is called *brazing*. There are certain metals that are not possible to join. Brazing solves that problem by using another material often a metal also which is more malleable than the 2 metals being joined together. This alloy is referred to as the *filler metal.*

Since there are many kinds of metal there are also many ways to braze differing metals together. Some of these variations in the brazing technique are:

1. *Torch Brazing:* The most common form of brazing is *torch brazing*. The preferred method of artists for creating metal sculptures since it is accessible for small scale production. Torch brazing can either be manual, automatic or machine generated.

   Manual torch brazing involves the use of a gas flame placed underneath or near the metal joints being placed together. It is a very specialized and labor intensive process.

   Automatic torch brazing, on the other hand, removes the human element in the process. It is great for mass production purposes. It delivers high quality brazed joints using industry grade brazing equipment. And it is the most cost efficient of the 3 torch brazing techniques.

   Machine torch brazing is a combination of manual and automatic torch brazing in that it requires both a human and machine element. A person monitors the process and adds alloy when the process requires it.

2. *Furnace Brazing:* The form of brazing that is used for large scale joint metal production. It is rare for artists to use furnace brazing as a technique for creating sculptures since acquiring the furnace for brazing is very expensive.

3. *Silver Brazing:* The brazing technique that uses silver as the filler material. The alloy that is placed in between two different metals so that they are joined together. Of all metal elements, available for brazing silver is the most congruent with all sorts of metals. Silver almost always can be brazed or be welded into any metal surface. This makes silver the filler material of choice for silver brazing.

4. *Vacuum Brazing:* The most expensive form of torch brazing because it requires a vacuum chamber vessel to braze metal joints together. *Vacuum brazing,* however, is known for its ability to deliver very clean, streamlined metal joints that are very strong and have very high integrity.

Forging

Forging is a metal sculpture technique that has been around for centuries. In the beginning, metal smiths would use hammer and anvil to forge or shape a metal into any form they want. In the 12th century hammer and anvil were replaced with the use of water powered equipment on a new form of metal called iron. In the advent of the industrial age the forge evolved into an actual facility that contained tooling, raw materials, products, forging equipment, and modern engineering processes to create all sorts of metal work.

Sculpting: 1-2-3 Easy Techniques to Mastering Sculpting

Today artists can forge any metal surface into many different shapes and sizes using power driven hammers and presses. Depending on the forging equipment it can either be powered by compressed air, steam, hydraulics or electricity.

Tools for Metal Sculpture

Here are some of the basic metal sculpture tools available to artists in the production of their art:

1. *Oxy-Acetylene Brazing Kit*: A set of oxy-acetylene powered gadgets which includes oxygen regulators, twin hoses, acetylene gauges, brazing tips, turbo torches and the like.

2. *Air & Steam compressors:* Industrial or art equipment that are used to compress excess air or steam and re-use or recycle them to power the compressor. Equipment or tool used to power hammers and presses to shape and forge metal.

3. *Automated hammers & presses*: Hammers and presses automated by either steam, air or water compressors to create clean and uniform metal shapes and forms.

4. *Turbo torch:* Nitrogen powered torch used to weld or braze metals together.

5. *Safety gear*: Sets of personal protective gear that covers important parts of the body or even the entire body while the artist is brazing, forging, or building a metal sculpture. Safety gears include hard hats, hand gloves, welding eyeglasses, ear guards, industrial boots, etc.

Chapter 5: Reproduction Techniques

Two of the most common reproduction techniques for sculptures are *molding* and *casting*. Molds and casts are important components to most sculpting processes, especially common with *modeled sculptures*.

A *master cast* is often a clay mold that is used to reproduce metal sculptures. The process goes something like this:

1. Liquid plaster is poured into a clay model.

2. Once the plaster has solidified into a mold it is cut in two. The clay model is removed.

3. After the mold is cleaned it is assembled back into a whole. It is filled with plaster, concrete or fiberglass resin.

4. The mold is chipped away or removed once the plaster or resin inside it has set and the final shape of the sculpture is created.

Molding

Flexible molds are the more cost efficient form of cast or molds available to a sculptor. Since they are flexible, it is possible to remove them from the final product without destroying them. They can then be re-used multiple times to create and reproduce the same shaped sculpture.

Flexible molds are great for mass produced and commercial pieces of sculptures. They are made from flexible materials such as gelatin, vinyl, and rubber. A nuance with flexible molds is it should be covered with a plaster case while it is being filled with plaster, wax, or resin. This is the best way for the flexible mold to retain its shape which is imperative for the final product.

Lost-wax process is the preferred method used by sculptors to build metal sculptures. It starts with creating mold made from wax. The wax mold, which is the master cast, is then covered by another mold often a pliable plaster mold which can generate the shape of the wax mold inside it. When the shape of the wax mold is set inside the plaster mold, heat is introduced into the plaster mold so that the wax mold is melted away.

This means there is a cavity inside the plaster mold left in the shape of the wax mold. This is when liquid metal is poured inside the plaster mold. Once the liquid metal solidifies inside the plaster mold, it is then opened to reveal the metal sculpture. The *lost-wax process* is the preferred method for generating very refined and polished metal sculptures.

Sand molding is the preferred method for sculptures that do not require very polished surfaces. The process is much the same with the lost-wax process except that instead of wax & plaster a special kind of sand is used to create the mold. Since the material is coarse sand the final sculpture usually has a coarse texture mimicking that of the sand mold.

Slip casting is the process of pouring liquid clay into a plaster mold. When the water from the liquid clay dries up and the clay has set into the shape of the plaster mold, it is removed from the plaster mold. It is then dried a bit more before it is fired up inside the kiln.

Tools for Molding

Some of the tools and materials used by artists for molding are:

1. *Molding plaster & mixing bowls:* The material used as base to create the shape or form of a mold is the molding plaster. Often these plasters are mixed in a plaster bowl.

2. *Magnifiers for detail work:* These are glasses that the artist can use to work on the minute detail of the artwork.

3. *Mold dividing shim:* A thin sheet of metal roll that is used to divide or separate chunks of mold plaster.

4. *Mold makers knife set:* A set of different kinds of molding knife used to cut, shape, dissect plaster mold in the process of creating the sculpture.

5. *Moulage:* These are the silicone, wax or gelatin based molds that are used to generate the shape, details, and texture of any part of the human body. Today *moulage* can be used to copy the shape or form of any material or object.

6. *Plaster carving chisel set:* A set of chisels that are used to carve the plaster into the shape or form the artist wants it to have.

Pointing

Another reproduction technique artists utilize to create sculptures is *pointing*. This requires the use of a pointing machine which has several arms and pointers. The pointing machine selects and marks the key points of a three-dimensional object and replicates that on a flat surface such as wood, concrete, stone, or metal. Once the points on the surface are marked using the pointing machine, the work on reproducing the same object can commence. The points are drilled first and then the mass or chunks of wood that are not required are cut off. This allows for the sculpting surface to acquire the basic shape of the sculpture.

Pointing machines are some of the most common equipment found in every sculpture project. These days they have evolved from manual to electric powered pointing machines.

Tools & techniques for Pointing

The main tool or equipment used for pointing is the pointing machine. The pointing machine consists of the following parts: calipers, metal rivets, the T-cross, the needle, carving tools, and drilling tools.

Chapter 6: Finishing Techniques

All sculptures go through the same finishing process. They are either given a natural finish or an applied one. *Natural finish* allows the surface to retain its original texture. On the other hand, *applied finish* often covers over the texture of the wood, stone or metal surface. This is the reason applied finishing on sculptures is either seen as a way of preserving or decorating the surface.

In this chapter, we will discuss the many forms of sculpture finishing techniques. They are polishing, painting, gilding, pagination, and electro-plating.

Polishing

The most common form of finishing for sculptures is *polishing and smoothing.* It is considered a natural form of finish because the original texture of the sculpture surface is not altered. Instead it is celebrated by polishing and smoothing the surface. The materials used for polishing are called abrasives.

There are a few abrasive materials available to every sculptor. These are whiting, pumice, emery, and sandstone. To make the most of these abrasives the stone surface is often wet before they are applied. The best way to polish hard stones is with the use of wax. It gives stones like granite and marble acquire a sleek high gloss finish.

Wood on the other hand uses a different kind of polishing abrasive. This most common wood abrasive is sandpaper. To smoothen and polish as well round off wood surfaces sandpaper is the best material to use. For the high gloss polish, linseed oil and beeswax are the most popular glossing components for wood.

Metal is another surface that has a special way of achieving polish. For metal sculptures, artists use steel wool and emery paper. To enhance the metal polish and make it more durable buffing wheels that are power driven are used to give any metal sculpture or surface a long lasting high gloss polish.

Tools for polishing

The basic tools often used in the polishing and smoothing of stone or wood metal sculptures are:

1. *Cotton polishing wheel set:* These are cotton tipped polishers often attached to a power-driven buffer used to clean up the surface of stone or metal sculptures.

2. *Diamond and carbide brazed tools:* These are rounded and flat steel or iron disks tipped or textured with diamond or carbide. They are often attached to a power-driven buffer tool and used to polish or create a certain finish to a stone surface.

3. *Buffing wheels:* These are power driven equipment where all sorts of polishing attachments are placed on for achieving an even and clean polish on stone, wood or metal sculptures.

4. *Steel wool & emery paper:* The most ubiquitous materials for polishing found in every artist's shop. Steel wool is great for polishing any surface. It is particularly favored for stone and metal. Emery paper is much the same as steel wool.

5. *Sandstone:* The preferred material used by artists throughout the centuries for polishing stone is sandstone.

6. *Wax:* To achieve that high gloss polish on any stone, metal and wood surface many forms or types of wax are used.

Painting

An applied form of finishing technique used to enhance the look and feel of a piece of sculpture is *painting*. If an artist for example wants a tree sculpture to look like a real tree it needs to be painted to look like a tree. Almost all kinds of surfaces used for sculptures can be painted on as a final step. Terra-cotta, stone, wood, even glass can be painted on. If a wood, stone or metal surface is properly prepared and primed paint can be applied to it.

Since painting is often the final step in the sculpting process, this is the stage where the artist is most involved in. Painting requires a lot of detail work that only the nuanced touch of an artist can provide. The artistic flare that allows a piece of sculpture to look as realistic or as artistic as it should. Sometimes it is even necessary to bring in painting specialists to ensure that the paint work is per the highest expectation set by the artist or the client.

Painting through the years has turned into the preferred finishing technique primarily because there has been so much improvement on paint technology. These days, a wide range of high-quality paint is available to every artist. Paint that enable artists to achieve the results desired for their sculptures.

Tools for Painting

The most common form of giving sculptures a proper finish is the application of paint. The tools and materials artists use to work with this technique are:

Sculpting: 1-2-3 Easy Techniques to Mastering Sculpting

1. *Industrial Brush set:* Every painting project requires a varied set of industrial paint brushes. These brushes will differ in brush length, width, material, and thickness. Artists often have a large array of both industrial and art brushes at their disposal.

2. *Paint Spray gun:* For an even finish, paint spray guns are often the preferred tool. Also, this painting tool enable artists to work at a much faster pace than paint brushes.

3. *Canvas drop cloth:* Canvas is often used to cover areas that are not supposed to be painted on or to protect the walls and flooring while the paint work on a piece of sculpture is ongoing.

4. *Detail brush set:* To get into the nook and crannies of a sculpture and to give surface texture to the paint on the sculpture surface detail brush sets are often utilized.

5. *Compressed air dryer:* Clean and dry compressed air is projected on the painted surface by the compressed air dryer. This allows the paint to dry in an even and clean manner. It allows the sculpture to have an even and dry paint finish in a matter of minutes.

6. *Paint roller set:* Much like the brushes, paint rollers are used to apply paint on the surface of the sculpture. Often, rollers are used on large scale sculptures.

Gilding

The process of adding a decorative layer of gold, silver or bronze leaf to a surface is called *gilding*. Before any sculptural surface can be inlaid with a thin layer of gold or silver leaf it should be properly primed first. Another term used for gilding one that is more familiar to people currently is *gold plating*.

The technique of gilding was first developed in ancient Egypt. Gold and silver was very much valued during the time of the pharaohs that the process of inlaying entire palaces with these valuable metals was a common occurrence back then. Gilding is an ancient art that has since been adopted by all artistic cultures of the world.

In fact, it has evolved into two distinct forms: Mechanical gilding and chemical gilding.

a. *Mechanical gilding:* This is the process of mechanically applying the gold leaf into a wood, metal or stone surface. With metal surfaces, silver or gold gilding is possible when the metal surface is first heated. The metal surface needs to be red hot for the silver or gold leaf to adhere to it. A mechanical burnishing tool is then used to place the gold leaf onto the hot metal surface. To finish it off cold burnishing acts as the final process.

To mechanically gild wooden surfaces, it is first coated with a thin layer of plaster of Paris or gesso. The gesso is then allowed to dry. Then the gesso surface is polished and smoothened. After which it is sprayed with water containing rabbit glue. This is referred to as *wet gilding*. Once the gesso surface is wet the gold leaf is placed on top of it and left to dry.

Another form of mechanical gilding for wood surfaces is *oil gilding*. The process is the same with water gilding except that linseed oil is applied on the gesso surface instead of water & glue. The gold leaf is placed on top oil coated surface and left to dry. If the artist wants a high gloss and very polished surface to a wood sculpture, *oil gilding* will be the preferred mechanical gilding method.

b. *Chemical gilding*: This finishing technique is a little bit more involved than its counterpart since it requires the gold or silver components to be combined with certain sets of chemical combinations.

1. *Cold Gilding*: Combining aqua regia with a solution of gold and dropping a linen rag into the chemical solution results in the linen getting burnt to a crisp. The heavy black ash that comes out of the process is then placed on a silver metal surface. By rubbing it down with either the finger or a piece of leather, the silver surface acquires a gold-plated finish.

2. *Wet Gilding*: This involves a combination of ether and gold chloride. Once the two elements are combined they are shaken and agitated. After which the mixture can settle and rest. The ether then rises to the surface after a certain time. The gold at this point is now fused with the ether. The mixture is then funneled with the intention of separating the gold infused ether from the acid.

   To plate iron or steel with the gold infused ether, which is the product of *wet gilding*, the metal surface is first brushed with a layer of emery or wine. Only then can the ether containing layers of gold in it is brushed onto the piece of steel or iron. As the ether dries the gold is retained on the metal surface.

3. *Fire Gilding*: A gilding technique that involves creating an *amalgam* of gold to be applied onto a metal surface to give it a golden finish is called fire gilding. The amalgam is prepared in this manner.

   Gold is reduced into thin grains or plates. The grains of gold are then heated to the highest temperature possible and once red hot they are dropped into heated mercury. Once smoke appears after the two elements have been combined it is stirred with an iron rod. This process allows the gold to be mixed in completely with the mercury solution.

The gold and mercury solution is then allowed to cool down. Once it is cold and can be handled, the amalgam of gold & mercury is placed in a chamois made of leather. The mercury is then pressed out of the amalgam by squeezing on the leather chamois. The gold in the form of a yellow buttery substance is retained in the chamois.

The metal surface the amalgam of gold is to be placed on should be checked first before the amalgam is applied to it. If the metal surface is wrought, then a thin layer of mercury needs to be brushed into its surface before the amalgam of gold is place on top. If the metal surface is plain, then no mercury coating is necessary.

The amalgam can be applied on top of it. The gold plate from the amalgam will only adhere to the metal surface if it is properly heated. Too much will make the gold evaporate and too little heat will not allow it to attach securely. Artists who use this technique understand the sensitivity of applying the amalgam of gold to a metal surface.

4. *Depletion Gilding*: A technique discovered by the Spaniards many centuries ago. *Depletion gilding* involves etching a metal surface with acid. This often results in a porous kind of gold surface. The textured gold surface is then polished or burnished which results in the metal acquiring a shiny gold surface. The technique is very effective. Metal pieces that go through *depletion gilding* look like they are authentic gold pieces.

Tools for Gilding

Gilding is an ancient and complex process of decorative art whose tools have also evolved and improved through the ages. Some of the most basic gilding tools are:

1. *Instacoll tool:* Every gold or silver gilding project uses the instacoll tool. It is a pencil shaped tool which has rubber tips on both ends. It allows the artist to apply gold leaf on the nooks and crannies of any surface without tearing the gold or silver leaf apart because of its rubberized tips.

2. *Gilders cushion:* Also, referred to as a gilder's pad. It is a wooden board covered in chamois leather and padded with felt. The gilder's cushion is used as a base for the manipulation of and cutting loose of gold or silver leaf in the process of gilding.

3. *Poliment brush:* Poliment is the material applied to any surface that will go through the process of gilding. The poliment brush is a very hard and

stiff brush that is used to clean the poliment surface in preparation for the application of the gold or silver leaf.

4. *Agate stones:* Another material used to prepare the surface which silver or gold leaf will be placed on are polished agate stones. Place on a buffing wheel tip the agate stone is placed in contact with the stone, wood or metal surface. It then polishes the surface so it acquires a smooth and even surface.

5. *Gilders knife:* Often a very sharp, high quality stainless steel knife used to remove or cut gold or silver leaf from the sculpture or the gilder's cushion.

6. *Drapery of horsehair:* Another material used to polish any surface in preparation for gilding is drapery of horsehair. It is a cloth with an abrasive surface perfect for surface polishing and smoothing.

7. *Repairing brush:* A small and thin tipped brush used for fastening or repairing the gold or silver leaf on the surface of a sculpture.

8. *Gilders brush set:* A set of brushes that is used for the application and transfer of silver or gold leaf onto a surface. Often the artist will brush the gilder's brush onto the surface of his skin before using it on a gold leaf. The natural oils present in human skin attaches itself onto the gilder's brush and when it is placed in contact with the very thin layer of gold leaf the oils allow the gold leaf to adhere easily to the gilder's brush.

9. *Fan brush:* To allow gold or silver leaf to attach more closely to the nooks and crannies of a sculpture the fan brush is the preferred tool.

10. *Silver or gold leaf:* The element that is used to achieve the gold or silver gild on the sculpture is silver and gold leaf. These are available in the form of rolls, think layers of leaf, or flakes.

Patination

A patina is a thin layer of color or texture that metal or wood surfaces acquire in time and through exposure to the elements. This is especially common in antiques. Patinas are prized because they add a layer of beauty to metal or wood pieces as well as protect it from rust and the damages of age.

Patination is the process of acquiring or adding a patina to a piece of metal surface. In sculptures, adding a patina is a great way to give the sculpture an aged look or add a layer of texture that adds to its aesthetic value.

When choosing *patination* as a finishing technique artists have three ways to achieve it:

1. *Acquired Patina:* The most natural way to let a piece of sculpture acquire a patina is by allowing it to *acquire the patina* through natural means. This is a bit of a lengthy process one that involves years to accomplish. It also involves making sure the piece of metal or wood sculpture is exposed to the right sulfur rich environment. The only environment that creates a layer of green patina on a metal and wood surface naturally.

2. *Applied Patina:* Another term for applied patina is *distressing*. This is the process of deliberately adding a look or layer of patina into a metal or wood sculpture. The purpose is often decorative. The artist wants the sculpture to have that antique and aged look.

    For bronze sculptures, patina is achieved when it is exposed to chlorides. This results in a green hue on the bronze surface. When exposed to sulfur compounds, bronze sculptures turn brown instead of green. On copper pieces, patina is achieved when vinegar or acetic acid is applied to the copper surface. Depending on the metal or wood surface there is compatible chemical element or compound that will allow it to get a patina of age.

3. *Repatination:* This process of adding a protective layer of patina is often used in antiques that have lost the original layer of patina it naturally acquires. This often happens when the antique piece is cleaned too often or buffed too often.

    Antiques are valued precisely because of the aged look or patina it has acquired through years of exposure to the elements. When the original patina of a piece of antique is reduced then so is its value. For an antique to keep on adding to its patina and therefore value it needs to retain or enhance its layer of patina.

    Repatination is a proven method antique dealers and collectors use to ensure that the patina of their antique pieces is retained and enhanced.

Tools for Patination

The tools for creating patina in antiques, the materials used that allow a piece of metal to look like it is a piece of antique are very basic. Materials such as cloth, brush, spray gun are often the most common tool options for patination or repatination.

The key component of every applied and repatination project is in the choice of chemicals used to achieve the patina. As mentioned earlier in the chapter, depending on the surface that needs to be patinated, the artist could either choose to use acetic acid or sulfur based compounds to create a layer of patina on any metal or wood surface.

Electro-plating

The finishing technique that uses electric currents to allow a metal layer to coat another metal surface is called *electro-plating*. The reason artists use electro-plating in sculptures is it allows them to change the surface of a metal object. Electroplating makes it possible for a copper surface to have a gold coating for example. Or it allows a silver surface to have a bronze surface. A metal surface can be changed into another metal surface using electro-plating.

In a way electro plating is much like gilding except that with electroplating, the process is much more complex involving the mixture of compounds and chemicals via electric current. Unlike gilding however, electroplating gives the artists a wider range of metal finishes for their sculpture not just silver or gold. And although electroplating is a more complicated process than gilding it is so much more inexpensive and allows the artist to apply it to a larger scale of sculptures.

Tools for Electro-plating

Since electroplating is a very involved chemical process, it is not a surprise that the tools and materials used for adding a different metal layer on another metal surface is numerous and complicated. And since electroplating involves mixing sensitive chemicals together it is always good to proceed with the process with caution.

Here are the basic tools:

1. *Anodes, Beakers, Plating Pens & Plating accessories:* Anodes are the most important component of the electroplating process. It is a pure piece of element that the artist wants to replicate. For example, if electroplating with gold then a 24K gold anode is required.

   Beakers are either made up of glass or stainless steel. Depending on the element being electroplated the choice of beaker is determined. If electroplating nickel for example it is better to use a stainless-steel beaker to create the element in.

   Then there are the electro-plating pens. These are the pen shaped tools that allow the artist to electroplate a metal surface. It involves having the pen, the metal element and the metal surface to be changed to meet each other. The electric current runs through the plating pen via the plating machine and it conducts the two metal elements together so that the initial metal element adheres to the original metal surface changing it to another metal layer.

2. *Plating solutions:* Since plating solutions are chemical based only professionals are allowed use and access to these solutions. Professionals

who are equipped with the skill and knowledge to handle the chemical plating solutions with care and caution. Some of the plating solutions available to professional artists in the market are – black antique plating solutions, nickel plating solutions, cyanide free gold plating solutions, and dry acid salt plating solutions.

3. *Electro-cleaning products:* These are the chemical solutions used for cleaning and polishing the electroplated metal surface. They are used in the final stage of the electroplating process where the metal surface has been changed already and it needs to be polished and cleaned. In much the same way with plating solutions, electro-cleaning products should be used and handled with extreme care.

4. *Electroplating kits:* These kits contain the basic tools and materials for electroplating. Anodes, beakers, plating pen, plating solutions and electro-cleaning solutions are all part and parcel of every electroplating kit. With it any artist should be able to proceed with electroplating any metal surface. These are not intended for large scale electroplating projects however. Kits can only electroplate a few metal pieces and surfaces at a time.

5. *Plating fume hoods:* A very important tool for electroplating is the plating fume hood. It is used to contain and control the fumes, which are often dangerous, emanating from the metal surfaces in the electroplating process. The fume hoods have exhaust channels where the plating fumes can travel to and are expelled far away from the artist and people conducting electroplating.

6. *Plating machines & rectifiers:* The electroplating machine is the apparatus that generates the electric current that allows metal to be electroplated on to another metal surface.

7. *Rhodium & Palladium plating solutions:* These are the sulfur acid based solution that generates a super-hard and clean metal finish on any metal surface. It is often used in cleaning and refurbishing gold jewelry. Rhodium and palladium solutions give any silver or gold surface an enhanced silver and gold finish. It makes any metal surface look brand new and polished.

8. *Safety gear:* These are sets of personal protective gear that covers important parts of the body or even the entire body while the artist is electroplating a metal sculpture. Safety gears include hard hats, hand gloves, eyeglasses, ear guards, industrial boots, etc. Protective gear is especially important for electroplating because hazardous chemicals are involved.

Conclusion

Thank you again for downloading this book!

I hope this book could help you to understand the very many sculpting techniques available out there. These are tried and tested techniques that every artist interested in creating sculptures can take on to create great art. These sculpting techniques have been developed and evolved through the ages by master artists, artisans and craftsmen located in every part of the world.

The next step after reading the book is to choose a sculpting technique that best suits the sculpture you would like to create. Based on the topics discussed in the book there is at least one technique at an artist's disposal to create the sculpture in mind.

Finally, if you enjoyed this book, please take the time to share your thoughts and post a review on Amazon. It'd be greatly appreciated!

Thank you and good luck!